Walter L. Simtou

Teapot Philosophy

Walter L. Simtou

Teapot Philosophy

ISBN/EAN: 9783337239305

Printed in Europe, USA, Canada, Australia, Japan

Cover: Foto ©Thomas Meinert / pixelio.de

More available books at **www.hansebooks.com**

Teapot ❦ ❦ ❦ ❦ Philosophy

WITH SUPPLEMENTARY THOUGHTS
AND SUGGESTIONS

A PLEA FOR PRACTICAL RELIGION IN PLAIN LANGUAGE FOR COMMON PEOPLE ❧

WALTER L. SINTON

Price 25 Cents

CHICAGO
Published by the Author
MDCCCXCIX

PREFACE.

Fellow seekers after truth, for the sole purpose of converting it, when found, into conduct, in presenting this little book for your perusal and earnest consideration, it is my sincere desire that you will not waste time in searching for literary merits, as there are none sought or claimed for it. All that I desire is, that the language may be found so plain, and the construction so simple, that the most ordinary intellects may grasp my meaning, and be utterly unable to twist my utterances to suit themselves.

The facts contained in the poem *Teapot Philosophy* were suggested by a Chinese teapot, which I was sending to my sister on the occasion of her wedding some ten years ago, as a token of my best wishes for herself and husband. I only intended to write a few lines expressing this, but the letter continued to grow as the gravity of the situation, not only for my relatives but also for myself, forced itself upon me.

One by one the facts and the difficulties inevitably issuing from them sternly and irresistibly presented themselves to me, and I was irresistibly impelled to record them. Several of these facts, and difficulties springing from them, stood out most prominently. These emphatically demanded immediate solution unless I concluded that I was insane and living in a world peopled by demented creatures and surrounded by hallucinations. Of the facts and difficulties which were suggested to me by the pot which contains the "cup that cheers but not inebriates," was first the doubt as to whether language has any definite meaning. I found that in reading from a book called the Bible, admitted by the majority of the English speaking people to be the rule of conduct, as well as in all other utterances professed as the rule of life, that black sometimes means white and *vice versa.*

One example of this, of which there are many, was the late war with Spain. This occurred between two nations confessedly Christian, and who take as their rule of conduct the Bible. In the Old Testament it is written, "Thou shalt not kill;" in the New Testament this is still more strongly emphasized in the following passages: "Resist not him that is evil;" "Love your enemies;" "Vengeance belongeth unto me; I will recompense, saith the Lord;" "If thine enemy hunger, feed him; if he thirst, give him drink: for in so doing thou shalt heap coals of fire upon his head." There are many other passages that could be quoted to the same end, but they are too numerous to mention, and can be easily recalled by almost anyone speaking English. Yet in spite of all these express commandments forbidding to kill, we find both nations actually beseeching the Author of these commands for assistance to slaughter each other.

The poet speaks truly when he writes that our modern disparity between profession and conduct is so great that "One murder makes a villain, millions a hero; numbers sanctify the crime." When I inquired as to the rule I was to apply to harmonize these inconsistencies, so that

I might judge accurately when black means white or the reverse, no one could tell me.

The second was, if white means black at one time and at another white, why not rewrite these rules and regulations for conduct, definitely stating when black means black and white black? To this also I found no solution. The result to a simple and honest mind was bewildering in the extreme.

The third that forced itself upon me was that the majority of people were living a treadmill life, and were not conscious of the fact. That this habit or routine governed their conduct, not what they professed to believe.

Now, the object in publishing the following poems or rhymed letters is to awaken people to this fact. So that when once aroused they may set to work and solve the problem, viz.: What should be the governing factor in all action? What should be the rule of conduct? If habit and feeling, then let us throw all profession of law and reason overboard and manfully confess that we are living according to our desires and habits. This logically would mean the survival of the fittest, irrespective of any supposed standard of right and wrong. Or else, make our desires and habits conform to the highest reason, which is law and the only true conscience.

Either of these positions would be honest and manly compared with the position we now take of sitting astride the fence, ready to jump down on whichever side suits us best for the moment.

If this book succeeds in aiding even one fellow being in reaching the true solution of these bewildering and vital difficulties, I am repaid for its publication.

John Ruskin on Modern Infidelity.

(From concluding chapter of "Modern Painters.")

"The form which the infidelity of England, especially, has taken, is one hitherto unheard of in human history.* No nation ever before declared boldly, by print and word of mouth, that its religion was good for show but 'would not work.' Over and over again it has happened that nations have denied their gods, but they denied them bravely. The Greeks, in their decline, jested at their religion, and frittered it away in flatteries and fine arts; the French refused their's fiercely; tore down their altars and broke their graven images. The question about God with both these nations was still, even in their decline, fairly put though falsely answered. 'Either there is, or is not, a Supreme Ruler; we consider of it, declare there is not, and proceed accordingly.'

"But we English have put the matter in an entirely new light: 'there is a Supreme Ruler; no question of it; only He cannot rule. His orders won't work. He will be quite satisfied with euphemisms and respectful repetitions of them. Execution would be dangerous under the existing circumstances, which He certainly never contemplated.'

"I had no conception of the absolute darkness which has covered the national mind in this respect until I began to come into collision with persons engaged in the study of economical and political questions. The entire naiveté and undisturbed imbecility with which I found them declare that the laws of the Devil were the only practicable ones, and that the laws of God were merely a form of poetical language, passed all that I had ever heard or read of mortal infidelity. I knew the fool had often said in his heart, there is no God; but to hear him say clearly out with his lips, 'There is a foolish God,' was something for which my art studies had not prepared me."

*This statement should include the English speaking race.—W. L. S.

TEAPOT PHILOSOPHY

-❧

Has Language No Definite Meaning ? A Plea for Practical Religion.

-❧

Thoughts Suggested by a Wedding Present.

-❧

"Speak thy truth if thou believest it,
    Let it jostle whom it may,
E'en although the foolish scorn it
    Or the obstinate gainsay;
Every seed that grows tomorrow
    Lies beneath the sod today."—MACKAY.

-❧

Sister, this souvenir I send to thee,
In memory of thy old-time love for tea;
And, though it may arrive a little late,
Take it for love, and never mind the date.
In winter evenings, when the blinds are down,
And fire bright, and toast is just done brown,
Take out this Chinese teapot, and what then?
Proceed to make a cup of tea for Ben.
And when you both have settled snugly round
Your little table, with its snowy ground
Of Irish damask, neatly garnished o'er
With toothsome dishes, an abundant store,
From out this teapot pour a cup apiece.

❧ Teapot Philosophy ❧

The soothing draughts will kindly thoughts increase.
Remember, then, how many have to roam
About the world, without a place called home.
Some without clothes except what's on each back,
And these, save name, most other virtues lack;
Of food and shelter ofttimes destitute,
And wanting these they soon lose all repute.
Convention eyes the poor men all askance,
Blames them, and pierces with the critic's lance;
Yea, though they be embodied decalogues,
Their fare is harder than the rich man's dogs';
For, lacking riches, what they've left counts naught,—
True Christian virtues are not sold, nor bought.
Such qualities are very little use
In gathering wealth, or even to produce
The commonest necessities of life:
To get these means hypocrisy and strife,
To cheat, to steal, and everything in fact,
Including lying, policy, and tact.
Yes, " business " is a synonym for these,
In spite of plausible and polished pleas.
Now men who make good bargains we applaud,
Although their weaker brethren they defraud.
Get wealth, get wealth; it is the world's great aim;
Get it, and few will criticise or blame,
Though in acquiring you have broken through
All laws of truth and justice, old or new.
Wealth is the God before which all men bow—

✈ Teapot Philosophy ✈

To gain it they will wallow like the sow;
For well they know, when they have gained its power
The world will on them every virtue shower;
Though they excelled the de 'il in all things base,
Their funeral sermons will be filled with grace.
These inconsistencies, my kindred dear,
Now that you 're entering on a wider sphere,
Should make you pause, consider, search and crave
To find solution of these problems grave.
First duty to yourselves, makes this demand,
Then those to come who will complete your band;
For with the law, "Increase and multiply,"
I 've not the slightest doubt you will comply.
Now to our fathers a great debt is due,
For liberties they gained for me and you
By martyrdoms and sufferings in *their* day,
And to our children we 've this debt to pay.
They were considered cranks and lunatics,
Imprisoned, exiled, stoned, abused with sticks.
Oft were they hungry, robbed of all they had,
Wasted by sickness, and with waiting sad;
Burned at the stake, beheaded on the block,
Whipped through the streets, put in the felon's dock,
Hanged on the gallows, tortured on the rack,
Their words perverted, actions painted black,
And with torn backs and lacerated sides
Dragged at the cart tail, whilst the mob derides.
For liberty their precious blood was spilled,

9

While with the love of man their souls were filled.
Ah, these their sufferings, were foundation stones,
Bound and cemented by their blood and groans;
Upon them is our present freedom based,
But with absurdities it's still encased;
Though liberty of conscience it bestows,
With leave to talk about our wrongs and woes,
Yet such a privilege is little good
To many millions, who, to get their food,
Must bow and cringe, and ask some power to give
Them leave to work for what they need to live.
Now of the larder those who hold the key
Can force the hungry to with them agree.
'T is said, "All things a man will give for life;"
Here lies the secret of most sin and strife;
And One who wrote of old again has said,
That "of the life of man the staff is bread;"
Therefore, before you tell men to be good,
Show them how honestly to get their food,
Which at the present time they cannot do.
This statement may appear untrue to you,
But if you'd knocked about the world like me,
With empty pockets, you'd begin to see
That practical religion, conscience pure,
Means poverty and hunger, "certain, sure."
In business life, religion put in force
Would bring as bad results as any curse:
Not that religion in itself is wrong,—

✼ Teapot Philosophy ✼

Its highest practice would make life a song.
To act and live it, and your larder fill,
Our present laws make quite impossible.
Until they're changed all preaching is in vain,
You must have rails on which to run a train.
The reason why I've written this to you,
Is thinking of what's likely to ensue:
The little ones that you will try to rear
In truth and honesty and godly fear.
Now should they take to heart the truths you teach,
And try to practice everything you preach,
Their life will bring them poverty, despair
(Unless you leave them wealth), a world of care.
They may become discouraged, and, alas,
Soon tramps and vagrants of the lowest class;
For circumstances change our course of life,
Our honesty and hopes, our power of strife,
And how the world appears to us, depends
Full much upon the color of our lens.
In church, who occupies a cushioned pew,
Will see the world in quite a different hue
From him, who, by the doorstep in the cold
Counts his few pence, as other men count gold.
What think ye would the noble Nazarene
Say to such sights as in our midst are seen?
Great churches, temples, meeting houses grand,
Six days within the week they idle stand,
While poor and homeless wander in the streets,

And at the empty breasts the baby greets.*
These structures built in honor of his name,
In which to preach his doctrine, spread his fame,
Who was the publicans' and sinners' friend,
And said, "To him who'd of thee borrow—lend."
The intimate acquaintance of the poor;
Too humble to rebuke the evil doer,
But simply told him, if the law he'd break,
The consequences be prepared to take;
For motives are the only gauge of acts;
He knew this, and he would not judge the facts.
Who blames a man for halting when he's lame
Forgets that in his case he'd do the same.
But all those looked upon as righteous *then*,
And, altogether, most religious men,
The teachers, priests, the scribes and pharisees,
Who loved in public place to bend the knees,
And lived according to the outward law,
To all appearances without a flaw—
These Jesus in his righteous anger cursed,
As of all criminals the very worst.
The rich man's chance of heaven seemed in his sight,
As of all others, most extremely slight.
I think few Christians hold this statement true,
Or else their rush for wealth we should not view;
Nor in the midst of plenty see men die
For want of nourishment they could not buy.
The highest law that's written in that book

*Cries.

'Gainst which a word the Christians would not brook,
Is, "See thou lovest thy neighbor as thyself;"
Yet they continue still to love their pelf,
And every law will cherish which sustains
Them in possession of their selfish gains.
Suppose before the judgment seat we stand,
And the Great Judge proceeds with this demand:
"These questions answer as your life you love
Or fear the vengeance of the powers above.
Superior faculties I gave to you,
From which much benefit there might accrue;
How have you used these powers 1 did bestow?
To help your brothers, or to cause them woe?
Think ye, your brains and powers I did increase,
The ignorant, meek and tender ones to fleece;
Forcing the little from them called their own,
To heap up riches for yourselves alone?
Perhaps you'll answer me like one of old,
'Do we our brothers keep?' in accents cold.
Again, I ask you all to answer, why
Will you pervert the truth and act a lie?
All you that are such sticklers for the law,
And say my testament's without a flaw;
Is it not written there, to help the weak,
The hungry feed, as well as truth to seek?
'Tis also said, do not oppress the poor;
That thou must not resist the evil doer,
But for all evil, good thou must return.

And for thine enemies thy love must burn.
With these commandments must your lives accord
Before you have the right to call me Lord.
How will you answer then these charges true?
By twisting all my words to suit your view,
And shouting glory, glory to my name,
To blind me, lest I see your selfish aim?
Or will you in your usual pompous style,
With patronizing air, nor look of guile,
Tell how you 've carried out my just decrees,
And even tried my slightest whim to please?
Of all the glorious works which you have done,
In words that something like what follows run:
'Lord, we 've done many works in thy great name;
With cannon, fire and sword we 've spread thy **fame,**
And made the red man listen to thy word;
Taught thy law good for evil with the sword.
We've sold them lots of Bibles and bad rum,
With other Christian virtues a good sum,
Through which thy doctrines have progressed so **well**
They've nearly all cleared out for heaven, or hell.
Then see what we have done for our own poor ;
Taught them it is thy will they should endure,
Nor grumble at our laws, howe'er unjust,
But while we fill our pockets, in Thee trust;
In heaven they will be sure of their reward
And six feet we'll give each body 'neath the sward.
Thou seest the earth's not big enough for all;
Thy architect did into error fall,

His calculations were somewhat astray
To meet the population of our day.
According to our wisest scientists,
Who prove it by both facts and figured lists,
That if humanity should propagate
Some centuries more, just at the present rate,
Mankind will then so overcrowd the earth
That they will cause a universal dearth
Of e'en the bare necessities of life—
While to get these would take continual strife,
Therefore we see the wisdom of thy plan
As all Thy wondrous works of love we scan;
How that in mercy thou did'st war ordain
With all the evils that make up its train,
Simply to thin the dirty, famished ranks
Of vulgar sinners and plebeian cranks,
Who teach that 'Love your neighbor as yourself'
Is higher than the love of place or pelf;
To clear away the wretched, loathsome crowd
Whose fancied wrongs forever cry aloud,
And almost try the patience of Thy saints
By their continuous, envious complaints:
Saying that 'We hard working, honest men,
So patient in our toil, are quick to ken
Sharp ways to take advantage of the weak,
Browbeat and trample in the dust the meek,
And make fast laws in favor of ourselves
To steal the produce from the man who delves,

The food and clothes from him whose horny hand
With sweated brow and sorrow, ploughs the land,
From sickly children, who in factories toil,
And men made brutes by working 'neath the soil
In cramped positions and in muddy light,
Until they almost lose their human sight.
The maidens, too, making their iron doom,
Nipped in the bud before they 've time to bloom;
Forced into motherhood before their time—
If such starved fruit could ever reach its prime—
In this condition to drag out their life,
A weary burden full of pain and strife.'
These charges, Lord, are all laid at our door,
With those not mentioned (twice as many more).
But well Thou knowest these are all absurd,
For it is written in Thy Holy Word—
The poor shall be with you unto the end,
'Tis useless then for us them to befriend;
To waste the riches Thou hast on us poured—
Reward for having always Thee adored,
While altering laws to give them back their own,
Would make untrue a mandate from Thy throne."
And now, dear hearts, this letter I must end,
With hope that you may fully comprehend
The few plain facts I have tried to write to you
In simple language, with no end in view
Like those who try the critic's ear to please
With words of music that your hearts might seize

✄ Teapot Philosophy ✄

And turn to any meaning you desire,
The modern Devil's ruse to quench God's fire,
Which was foretold by those who wrote of old
In language plain, unvarnished, rude and bold,
That in the latter days to calm their fears,
Men would buy teachers who could please their ears.
Now take and share these burdens of my heart,
Sternly, with love, make others bear their part,
Until the day when justice is fulfilled
And love has every quaking conscience stilled.
I little thought a teapot could suggest
So many thoughts of error and unrest,
But now that it has done so much for me,
Just let it do the same for Ben and thee.

What J. L. Spalding, Bishop of Peoria, Says.

"We must look, as educators, most closely to those sides of the national life where there is the greatest menace of ruin. It is plain that our besetting sin, as a people, is not intemperance or unchastity, but *dishonesty*. From the watering and manipulating of stocks to the adulteration of food and drink, from the booming of towns and lands to the selling of votes and the buying of office, from the halls of Congress to the policeman's beat, from the capitalist* who controls trusts and syndicates to the mechanic who does inferior work, the taint of dishonesty is everywhere. We distrust one another, distrust those who manage public affairs, distrust our fixed will to suffer the worst that may befall rather than cheat or steal or lie. Dishonesty hangs, like mephitic air, about our newspapers, our legislative assemblies, the municipal government of our towns and cities, about our churches even, since our religion itself seems to lack the highest kind of honesty, the downright and thorough sincerity which is its life breath."

*More scientifically speaking, the monopolist.

A PLEA FOR HUMANITY.

-●

"My ear is pained.
My soul is sick with every day's report
Of wrong and outrage with which the land is filled.
There is no flesh in man's obdurate heart;
He does not feel for man; the natural bond
Of brotherhood is severed as the flax
That falls asunder at the touch of fire."

-●

Men! O men! you must be sleeping, that you stand so
    idly by,
While young mothers age with working, and with hun-
    ger children cry.
Where's your manhood? where's your virtue? where's
    the freedom that you boast?
To let millions die from hunger while the corn's shipped
    from your coast;
Sold to keep some selfish landlord, living in luxurious
    ease,
Thus do rich men make you victims of unjust and vile
    decrees.
Not with love pay you this tariff, as for value you've
    received;
Loath you are, as though some robber of your money
    you'd relieved.

❧ A Plea for Humanity ❧

Light, and air, and earth, and nature, heritage of every
man,
This without respect of persons, or despotic scheme or
plan,
That by strength that's sometime mental, or more brutal that of arm,
Overrides the weaker natures, and oppresses to their
harm;
Doing despite to their birthright, which proclaims them
all free born,
Free and equal to each other, from no privilege fore-
sworn.
Thus all nature's gifts are common, common to us one
and all;
But when we monopolize them, then our brothers we
enthrall.
But let every man and brother do his share in each
day's toil,
Each in his own occupation drawing wages from the
soil;
Making rich and rare productions, every man after his
kind;
So they'll find their new creations suit each other's turn
of mind.
Then, with pleasure they'll exchange them, and it tends
to mutual gain;
What is got by man's exertion seldom gives his brothers
pain.

❧ A Plea for Humanity ❧

If superior strength producing should outdo our puny
throes,
We've no room to envy greatness when our small cup
overflows.
And the great cup thus producing, when it does o'erflow
its brim,
Droppings from it falling on us will refresh each weakly
limb.
But our boasted civilization makes each one a legal
thief,
And one thief will dupe another; so it always ends in
grief.
What a man has never wrought for he's no right to
call his own;
And if rent for nature's free gifts is reward for having
sown,
Sense and justice have no meaning, and all men are
arrant fools;
They'd much better die at once than be down-trodden
by such rules.
There's no law in earth or heaven that would warrant
" might as right,"
For it is a bestial nature, not for man whose wider
sight
Gives him knowledge of the uses that employ both great
and small
To their mutual advantage, when one does not covet
all.

❧ A Plea for Humanity ❧

Land is plenty, labor's plenty; there's no need that we
should starve,
And let landlords, speculators, from our produce fortunes
carve.
Rouse yourselves! Be up and stirring! Float true freedom's banner high;
Don't sit whining over evils you yourselves can rec-
tify.
Ye are like men bound in prison, that by some mesmeric
power
Still believe that they are freemen, while the lash yet
makes them cower.
Ye are mocked by a false title that contains for you no
rights:
Better be a slave in title, and not feel how hunger
bites.
You have nought but name to boast of, and it makes a
sorry meal;
Will it clothe your aged mothers, or make cold less
bitter feel?
Ye had better ponder o'er this; better put your wits to
work;
Use the reason nature gave you, from its promptings
never shirk.
May the cries of countless millions who in poverty have
died,
Through the laws of ruthless tyrants who all righteousness deride,

❧ A Plea for Humanity ❧

Join in one continuous volume of seething liquid fire,
That will surge through every fibre of mankind, from
    son to sire;
Till brute brains become so quickened that they under-
    stand aright,
That when reason governs feeling, and with love they
    both unite,
Then they'll see brute force is madness and has no con-
    vincing proof,
But adds bitterness to bitterness, and reason stands
    aloof.
And many who'd have joined our ranks if patiently
    persuaded
By logic so convincing that it could not be evaded,
While they behold some devilish deed whose violent
    display
Might have killed a thousand innocents, it fills them with
    dismay;
And they turn their backs upon us for deluded lunatics,
Think what fine ideas of justice, that need bombshells,
    stones and sticks;
Not by such barbaric warfare will we ever free the
    land,
For in "labor against rental" reason holds the winning
    hand.
Then no use we have for cannon, bombshells, guns or
    dynamite;
With united power invincible, derived from higher light,

✄ A Plea for Humanity ✄

We'll march into our heritage on the day that we
    agree,
And we'll hold it ever after as our day of jubilee,
The day in which our title is no mockery of fate,
For we'll hold as one community the land in every
    state.
Then, to call a man a landlord will be reckoned an
    insult,
In remembrance of the misery that from it did result.
In this great world-wide republic there'll be food for
    great and small,
And the babies will be welcomed as a benefit to all:
For every pair of hands and feet that are born upon
    the earth
Will be so much wealth of labor to provide against a
    dearth.
And their work will be congenial, not like an imposed
    task,
Just as easy as to flowers that in nature's sunshine bask.
Then they'll prove the " Malthus theory " is but an
    idle tale,
For when nature does outdo herself she knows how to
    curtail.
But the prospect is so dim and vague that aeons will
    roll by,
Many a million generations will live and work and die,
Before there is the slightest need that man should face
    this problem,

❧ A Plea for Humanity ❧

Though God in jest created men, of food and life to
  rob them.
Then we'll see no more the starveling wandering through
  our wintery streets,
Nor the poor abandoned woman whom the world with
  hardness greets;
For a charity unbounded, seldom known in this our day,
Will unfurl its royal banner and o'er mankind hold its
  sway.
We'll not want for emulation when all poverty shall
  end,
We can compete with one another, our own defects to
  mend.
Then the thief will be unknown and the murderous
  spirit dead,
For prenatal culture 'll have fair play and men will be
  well-bred.
Yes, beautiful as history says the old Greek heroes were,
For they studied form and culture with the greatest
  taste and care;
Had their ideal been but higher, not all for wasting
  war,
Then they might have reached the acme that the noblest
  men look for.
We've a chance to win the glory of ushering in the
  age
So oft foretold in rhyme and story, by prophet, priest
  and sage.

The just and poor have always longed for the coming
of the day
That will give all men an equal right to labor and fair
pay.
Then let's think and work in earnest, looking all around
the land,
Where we'll see distress and poverty widespread on
every hand,
And willing hearts and dexterous hands living a pauper's
life,
With young hopes blasted, ideals crushed, by the unequal
strife;
For 'tis not on skilful labor or intellectual worth
That the world bestows her bounties, or brings golden
tribute forth,
But for bulldog inhumanity that grips its victim's throat,
Or cunning, fox-like treachery, that o'er friends can grin
and gloat.
These tread under foot all justice, making honest men
their slaves,
And self respecting laborers but low, obsequious knaves.
So, by stealing hard earned wages till we feel how hunger
gnaws,
Strong wills are broken and free souls tamed to keep
their evil laws.
And the names, "Liberty" and "Justice," that once meant
something pure,
An embodiment of power and love that would all evils cure,

❧ A Plea for Humanity ❧

Have become but standing bywords, at which all men
    laugh and mock,
For they see they're but for rich men to protect their
    ill-gained stock,
And a hardened crew called "lawyers," who are paid to
    twist the truth,
Who upon their brothers' weaknesses grow fat and full,
    forsooth,
For they scoff at truth and purity as so much ranting
    cant;
Ah, well they know, where *these* hold sway their living
    is but scant.
Now strict honesty is looked upon as acting the fool's
    part,
And to steal and keep a million is considered " wise " and
    " smart."
He who succeeds in doing this is crowned with fame and
    glory,
And, if he should endow a church, the preachers laud
    in story.
Society's great premium is for him who has learned to
    steal,
It matters not what she may profess in words to think
    or feel.
Should less 'cute or weaker brother steal a spoon or dollar
    bill,
We imprison him for punishment, for lacking thieving
    skill.

❧ A Plea for Humanity ❧

Perhaps goaded on to madness by the direst sort of
    need,
And cold shouldered by his neighbors, who his prayers
    would never heed,
He broke through the tyrant bondage which ignorant
    souls benight,
Taking but a few small morsels that he felt were his
    by right.
For promiscuous hospitality the rich men do not care,
Though they have a chance of entertaining angels un-
    aware,
They fear such pure and holy spirits might prove un-
    pleasant guests,
By stirring up grim, ugly thoughts in their luxurious
    nests.
Of true and liberal maxims no longer men take thought,
For the greed of gold has warped their minds and their
    whole beings fraught.
Now the standard of success in life is "how pans out
    the gold,"
For the honest one of righteousness, has long grown
    worn and old.
They have no regard for honor now like what they
    used to have,
In dubious work 't is *business* that men use for conscience'
    salve.
"A good bargain" 's how they speak of it when they
    their neighbors rob,

✎ A Plea for Humanity ✎

By means of many a deep-laid scheme and low, deceitful
    job.
Ignorance and simplicity make rich harvests for the
    rogue,
Take advantage of necessity's the law that's now in
    vogue.
Nature's laws are so perverted that to win the simplest
    crown,
Means to trample on one's brothers and relentless beat
    them down.
And our women-folk a bondage bear worse than the
    southern slave;
He had property protection which tries wear and tear
    to save;
But *they* to the highest bidder are knocked down without
    reprieve,
The rich man's doll or popinjay, a badge upon his sleeve.
Driven to living slavery by the poverty bugbear,
For they are brave and dauntless spirits to face it that
    would dare.
This the reason why the money wins amongst the
    fairer sex,
That they choose a hollow, loveless life, lest need their
    souls should vex.
If they in young love's heated glamour should share the
    poor man's lot,
Experience shows young love oft flies through the win-
    dow from his cot;

A Plea for Humanity

For there poverty breeds carking care, and sickness swells
the list,

With a growing, pressing labor, that seems never to
desist;

This dulls the mind and senses, and the spiritual growth,

And the hopelessness of mending it inclines a man to
sloth;

It embitters all his life and thoughts, and love grows very
dim,

Till in fierce despair he curses God for ever making him.

Worry makes him hard and surly, and with all things
discontent;

Then upon his patient, slaving wife, he gives his feelings
vent;

And should he turn vicious, brutal, such are matrimony's
laws,

They give him power to do such deeds as would make
a savage pause.

He can kill her by slow torture in a thousand different
ways,

To which sudden death is mercy, and when done to
beasts earns praise.

The law gives her body to him, and he would control her
mind,

Yea, e'en her soul, her higher self, if he could the power
but find.

Great man! In his pride and self-conceit, he struts about
and strides.

❧ A Plea for Humanity ❧

He thinks he has superior gifts and poor womankind
derides,
Just as though she were a painted toy invented for his
use,
For his pleasure, whim or fancy, at his will to bind or
loose.
Now correlatives imply each other, say logicians wise,
And the oak or acorn which was first, an unsolved
problem lies.
In this day of light and culture which gives impartial
sight,
No one has proved that man o'er woman should hold
an owner's right,
For the man implies the woman, and she just as much
the man;
They're proclaimed by nature equal in the universal plan.
If woman seldom leads the race, 'tis because she's had
no chance,
And no doubt when solid justice reigns will often lead
life's dance.
Then, so much for our fair helpmeets; we must turn to
other themes,
Revealéd by the piercing light of love's ever searching
gleams,
To him who would obey the law, the ancient Golden
Rule,
To love your neighbor as yourself, though you may be
dubbed a fool.

Now plagiarists most preachers are, viewed beneath love's
    burning rays;

They live upon the fruits of toil, singing but oppressive
    lays.

Quoting the words of other men who their own expe-
    rience told;

Let them copy these, not quote, and speak their own
    lives open, bold;

By what power they've fought and conquered, moved
    and acted on what grounds;

If they have not this to tell us, sermons are but empty
    sounds.

Something personal and living is what's wanted now-a-day,

Present God and present devil not all based on old
    hearsay.

Then our mission to the heathen, when about our street
    they roam:

Mockery of true religion; charity begins at home.

Our concern about brute creatures, how they suffer from
    abuse,

Turning from our fellow beings, with deaf ears and
    hearts obtuse.

Sometimes from our stolen riches give a crumb to those
    who moan,

Then we look for praise and glory, for returning them
    their own.

Hospitals we have for sick men, homes for foundlings,
    waifs and strays,

Trying to appease our conscienee with the hypocrite's
displays.
Yet 'tis written on the pages of the volume we affect,
Through the needle's eye the camel will its passage make
direct,
Easier than the man with riches enter into peace and
rest.
Surely now, man's life and actions show he thinks this
only jest.
See what leagues and combinations, what emotional
crusades,
Men continually are making as the great Jehovah's aids,
In hopes to kill the tree of sin by lopping off the
branches,
Just like a maniac who would stop the Alpine ava-
lanches.
These fights are futile and absurd, as the laws of nature
show;
When boughs are lopped from off a tree, life will to the
others flow;
Causing them to bear such fruit old crops will drop into
the shade;
When you want to kill the tree, destroy the roots and
it will fade.
Now, the tree that we've to cope with is gigantic in its
growth;
Can't be balked in its fruition as we bind men by an
oath,

❧ A Plea for Humanity ❧

For its roots are deep and ancient, many fibred, tough
and strong;
From them spring in this world's systems all the phases
men term "wrong:"
Lying, drunkenness and sickness, with their colleagues,
murder, theft,
Want of food for brain and body of which millions are bereft.
These the vile fruits of that great tree whose true name
is selfishness,
Its life sustained on " might is right," stolen clothes its
flaunted dress.
And they who flourish by this tree, they are termed
" successful men;"
They are worshiped, praised and fêted like to gods who
all things ken.
Proud they turn upon their victims, blame them much
for being poor,
They, the wolves who stole their riches; oh how long
will men endure?
These are oft termed Christian heroes, say to Him they
bend the knee,
Who advocated on the Mount justice quite impartially.
And whose mighty follower said, " If you would the
gospel preach,
First feed the hungry, help the weak, then the truth
begin to teach."
I beseech you O my brothers, my hard worked and ill
paid friends,

❧ A Plea for Humanity ❧

All from selfishness who suffer, or the misery that it
   sends,
Think of what I've tried to tell you, with the words at
   my command,
Thoughts so true they've burned within me, burned till
   I could not withstand;
So I've had to give them utterance in my feeble, simple
   way,
Craving it may stir your spirits, till you rise in full
   array,
Compelled by love unbounded, it by divinest reason ruled,
Determined to change the system that so long has you
   befooled.

"ORTHODOX CHRISTIANITY."

Why it is looked upon with loathing and contempt, and avoided as a dangerous and subtle enemy by the poverty-stricken, and the thoughtful portion of the laboring classes.

" I do not see in Christianity the mystery of the incarnation, but the mystery of social order—the association of religion with " Paradise," an idea of equality which keeps the rich from being massacred by the poor.   An inequality of fortunes could not exist without religion.   A man dying of starvation alongside one surfeited with the world's goods would not submit to this difference unless he had some authority which assured him that in the future, and throughout eternity, the portion of each will be changed."

—Napoleon.

"Prejudices are to be destroyed, not tolerated." –Winwood Reade.

Landmarks on the Road to Truth

With Instructions by One
Who has Traveled the Road

IN recommending the following list of books, the literateurs' standpoint of style has not been considered, as it is held to be of secondary importance—the matter to be expressed is the first thing to be emphasized, and the style the second. The object in view in advising the study of these works is that they express truths of practical utility in the creating of perfect men and women. If we can get these truths well expressed from the academical point of view, and the people cultured enough to understand them from that standpoint—good—but if not, we must take them as we can get them and give them to others in the form that they can understand. These books are chapters in the grand book which contains the Science of Life, or the process of making perfect men and women. An understanding of the truths contained in them will solve the riddle of the Sphinx. At first sight they appear to conflict, but on closer inspection there will be found in the main a perfect harmony throughout. Each book delineates a brick in the grand edifice, but alas! oftentimes the author thought his brick the only one in the building, and was blind to the others, and in so far as he was so limited, his brick is imperfect and misleading.

Neither is it to be understood that in emphasizing these books, we believe them to be the only books worthy of being read; what we do know is that a perusal of them will naturally lead to the reading of other books along the several lines treated of by those in the category. Whether the readers find other authors who deal with the subjects in better or worse style, more lucidly or the reverse, depends not so much on any absolute standard by which such matters are judged, as the individual training and natural predilection of each reader. It is a law—we can never see but what we are; everything we look at reflects back our own image.

Anyone reading these works, to thoroughly comprehend the meaning of the Great Book, must take as a motto, "The Truth at *Any Cost.*" They must not be in love with any preconceived idea, habit, custom, or be swayed by their feeling or temperament. Let them, like a medical student, thoroughly dissect every subject that comes before them, irrespective of whether it is personally offensive or not. If they cannot do this, they need never hope to attain to the Truth. In the recommending of these books, not only is the effect they will have on the individual student held in view, but also the fact that they will give a knowledge of the proper book to place in the hands of the seekers after truth, in any of its multitudinous branches and at any stage of development. We must not forget that the people that have to be dealt with represent almost every age in the world's history in their individual development, as well as many grades in the educational attainments of the present day—from the grossest ignorance and narrow-mindedness to that of the highest culture, and the presentation of the same truth that will reach one stage or grade will be entirely refused by the other as non-comprehensible. The true teacher speaks to each class in its own language and from its own platform. Remember, "All things to all men that I may by all means save some," and "All things are lawful for me but not all things are expedient, all things are lawful for me, but I will not be brought under the power of any."

—⚭—

BREAKING GROUND.

"The man that is not moved at what he reads,
That takes not fire at their heroic deeds,
Unworthy of the blessings of the brave,
Is base in kind, and born to be a slave."

Even As You and I..B. Hall
Teapot Philosophy.............................Walter L. Sinton
Who Lies?...................................Blum & Alexander
Between Caesar and Jesus.............Prof. Geo. D. Herron

THE LAW (ECONOMICS)—Light Literature.

'He that gathers wealth to give to the poor his memory shall be fragrant as roses; but he that toils with the poor so that there be no poor, all the flowers of the garden cannot measure his sweetness."—ARAB PROVERB

Joshua Davidson, or a Modern Imitation of Christ...Linton
Alton Locke...............................Charles Kingsley
Yeast....................................Charles Kingsley
Caesar's Column.........................Ignatius Donnelly
Looking Backward................................Bellamy
Equality.......................................Bellamy
John Ball's Dream...........................William Morris
My Religion......................................Tolstoi
Almost Persuaded...........................Will N. Harben

38

"Ill fares the land, to hastening ills a prey,
Where wealth accumulates and men decay."
—*Goldsmith.*

The eloquent Patrick Henry said: "We can only judge the future by the past." Look at the past! When Egypt went down, two per cent. of her population owned ninety-seven per cent. of her wealth. The people were starved to death. When Persia went down, one per cent. of her population owned the land. When Babylon went down, two per cent. of her population owned all her wealth. The people were starved to death. When Rome went down, 1800 men owned all the known world.

How is it with the United States? Will we add it to Patrick Henry's list of countries ruined by the concentration of the wealth produced by all the people, into the hands of a few, while the many are starved?

Is the following prophecy of Lincoln, written to his friend Elkins, in Illinois, 1864, coming true?

"As a result of the war, corporations have been enthroned, and an era of corruption in high places will follow, and the money power of the country will endeavor to prolong its reign by working upon the prejudices of the people until all wealth is aggregated in a few hands and the republic is destroyed. I feel at this moment more anxiety for the safety of my country than ever before, even in the midst of war. God grant that my suspicions may prove groundless."

Let us study the following statistics taken from the U. S. census of 1890, and see.

WEALTH PRODUCED IN U. S. AND WHO GETS IT.

YEAR.	WEALTH.	PRODUCER PER CENT.	MONOPOLIST PER CENT.
1850	$ 8,000,000,000	62 1-3	37 1-2
1860	16,000,000,000	43 3-4	56 1-4
1870	30,000,000,000	32 2-3	67 1-3
1880	48,000,000,000	24	76
1890	62,000,000,000	17	83

TABLE APPROXIMATELY SHOWING THE MASSED CONCENTRATION OF INCORPORATED WEALTH IN ONE LIFETIME, WHICH HAS NO PARALLEL IN THE WORLD'S HISTORY OF EXPLOITATION.

	FAMILIES.	AMOUNT.
Princes of Wealth................	60	$ 3,000,000,000
Multi-Millionaires & Millionaires	24,940	29,750,000,000
Middle Class—Easy..............	1,244,015	15,000,000,000
PRODUCING CLASSES.		
Business Strugglers.............	3,899,586	12,000,000,000
Laboring Class..................	6,594,796	2,746,000,000

According to these statistics the present monopolistic system of production and distribution has concentrated seventy-one per cent. of the nation's wealth into the hands of nine per cent. of the population, and the process of concentration is still going on with accelerated rapidity.

A GLANCE AT THE CONCENTRATION OF ENORMOUS WEALTH INTO THE HANDS OF A FEW PERSONS.

Control of *$12,000,000,000* is held by 3,987 multi-millionaires. To comprehend its immensity we have only to remember that the combined wealth of twelve of our great States does not exceed *$7,000,000,000*. In the city of New York alone there are three men whose combined wealth exceeds *$500,000,000*. Ten men have acquired within a few years $790,000,000. *Sixty non-producing families hold more of the national wealth than 6,594,796 families* of the wealth-producing working classes. One family controls one-third of the railway system of the United States. The railroad companies hold land enough to make six states like Ohio. Mr. Disston, of Pennsylvania, holds 4,000,000 acres; Vanderbilts, 2,000,000 acres; Standard Oil Company, 1,000,000; Murphy, of California, a tract large enough to make a state the size of Massachusetts. The Schenly estate receives an annual income of $1,000,000. Viscount Scully holds 3,000,000 acres. The English nobility hold 20,000,-

40

Heavy Literature.

" With your science and your books
And your theories about spooks,
Did you ever hear of looking in your heart?
I didn't mean your pocket, Mister; no;
I mean that, having children and a wife,
And ten a week on which to come and go,
Isn't dancing to the tabor and the fife.
When it doesn't make you drink,
By Heaven! it makes you think,
And notice curious items about life."

Merrie England.................(*Nunquam*) R. Blatchford
Reply to Merrie England...(Ed. *Financial Almanac*) Callie
Social Problems...........................Henry George
Land Question................................. " "
Passage at Arms............................. " "
The Condition of Labor..................... " "
Progress and Poverty........................ " "
Protection and Free Trade.................. " "
Perplexed Philosopher...................... " "
My Dictatorship..............................
Outlines of Post's Lectures, Illustrated...................
Natural Taxation...................Thomas G. Shearman
New Economy.....................Lawrence Gronlund
Co-operative Commonwealth............Lawrence Gronlund
Communism..............................By a Capitalist
The Chicago Martyrs; Their Speeches in Court.........
Social Evolution...................................Kidd
New Republic...................................Schelhous
Ancient Lowly..................................Ward
Six Centuries of Work and Wages..............T. Rogers
The Land Question .. ..Fisher-Birbeck
Nationalization of Land.................Prof. A. R. Wallace
Law of Civilization and Decay...............Brooks Adams
England's Ideal.........................Edward Carpenter
Wealth Against Commonwealth............... H. D. Lloyd
Labor Copartnership.......................H. D. Lloyd
Wagner's Ring of the Niebelungen.............David Irvine
History of Socialism...............................Kirkup
Catholic Socialism.................................Netti
Genesis of the Social Conscience..................Nash
Facts and Forces...................Washington Gladden
Social Theory ....Bascom
Present Distribution of Wealth in U. S..........C. B. Spahr
Studies in Economics.........................Wm. Smart
The Workers. East and West............... Prof. Wyckoff
A Handbook of Socialism..........................Bliss
Science of the Millenium........Stephen and Mary Maybell

41

ooo acres. Mr. Rockefeller is computed to be worth 7,000,-
ooo more than the total wealth of the state of South
Carolina. In 1860 farmers owned one-half of the wealth
of the United States. In 1890 they owned less than one-
fifth.   —*From J. W. Arnold's Chart.*

The Social Revolution is bound to come. It will come
either in full panoply of law, and surrounded with all the
blessings of peace, provided the people have the wisdom to
take it by the hand and introduce it betimes;—or it may
break in upon us unexpectedly, amidst all the convulsions
of violence, with wild disheveled locks, and shod in iron
sandals. Come it must, in one way or the other. When I
withdraw myself from the turmoil of the day and dive into
history, I hear distinctly its approaching tread.—*Lassalle.*

"We can find no evidence of a holier spirit or a more
divine one in the Church than in any other human institu-
tion for the propagation of instruction. The Church has
never been superior to the times, never as far advanced as
the best men of the day, never a leader, but rather an op-
poser of progress; hindering when ideas were new, and
only coming in to help when workers without had proved
their discoveries, and it was evident that credit would be
lost by refusing to recognize them. There is no cruelty
the Church has not practised, no sin it has not committed,
no ignorance it has not displayed, no inconsistency it has
not upheld, from teaching peace and countenancing war to
preaching poverty and piling up riches. True, there have
been saints in the Church; but there have been great saints
out of it. Saintliness comes of conscientiously cultivating
the divine in human nature; it is a seed that is sown and
flourishes under the most diverse conditions."
                                —*Sarah Grand.*

"Here lie I, Martin Elginbrodde:
 Hae mercy o' my soul, Lord God;
 As I wad do, were I Lord God,
 And ye were Martin Elginbrodde."
                        —From *David Elginbrod.*

42

ICONOCLASTIC (THEOLOGICAL)—Light Literature

"For modes of Faith let graceless zealots fight;
His can't be wrong whose life is in the right."—POPE.

Robert Elsmere......................Mrs. Humphrey Ward
John Ward, Preacher....................Margaret Deland
John Inglesant............................John Shorthouse
The World of Cant.................................
Hypatia......................................Charles Kingsley
Lost Atlantis............................Ignatius Donnelly
Ragnarok.............................. " "
The Pilgrim and the Shrine....................E. Maitland
The Story of an African Farm...................Ralph Iron

Heavy Literature.

"Try all things; hold fast to that which is good."

"By the light of burning heretics Christ's bleeding feet I track,
Toiling up new Calvaries ever with the cross that turns not back.
And these mounts of anguish number how each generation learned
One new word of that grand Credo which in prophet-hearts hath burned
Since the first man stood God-conquered with his face to heaven up-
turned."—LOWELL.

Age of Reason...T. Paine
Ingersoll's Works....................................
Conflict between Religion and Science.........Prof. Draper
Martyrdom of Man........................Winwood Reade
Volney's Ruins...
Orbs of Heaven............................O. M. Mitchell
Literature and Dogma....................Matthew Arnold
The Childhood of the World ....E. Clodd
The Birth and Growth of Myth................... "
The Childhood of Religion......................... "
Story of the Creation; a plain account of evolution "
Lux Mundi ....
Paradoxes..................................Nordau
Conventional Lies of Our Civilization.............. "
Christianity and Agnosticism; a controversy between Prof.
    Thos. H. Huxley and others............................
Bible Myths and Their Parallels in Other Religions........
False Claims of the Church...............John E. Remsberg
Sixteen Crucified Saviors................. .....Kersey Graves
Christian Absurdities...........................John Peck
How to Study Strangers by Temperament, Face and Head.
    ....Nelson Sizer
Self Instructor in Phrenology........O. S. and L. N. Fowler
How to Read Character... ....R. S. Wells
Up to Date Home Study. Your Head and What Is In It.
    ....Mary E. Vaught.

" Without the love there would be no home; without the poverty no hell. Neither lightens the burdens of the other: each multiplies all that is terrible in both."

—*Helen H. Gardener.*

" So long as there shall exist, by reason of law and wisdom a social condemnation which in the face of a civilization that artificially creates hell on earth and complicates a destiny that is divine, with human fatality; so long as the *three problems of the age*—the *degradation* of *men* by poverty, the *ruin of women* by starvation and the *dwarfing* of *childhood* by physical and spiritual night—are not solved; so long as in certain regions social asphyxia shall be possible; in other words and from a yet more extended point of view, so long as ignorance and misery remain on earth, *books like these* cannot be useless."— *Victor Hugo.*

" The human race
To you means, such a child, or such a man,
You saw one morning waiting in the cold.
All's yours and you
All colored with your blood, or otherwise
Just nothing to you. Why I call you hard
To general suffering. A Red-haired child
Sick in a fever, if you touch him once,
Will set you weeping. But a million sick,
You could as soon weep for the rule of three."

" Woman, with her emotional nature morbidly stimulated by a vicious education of repression and concealment, keeps the world back in the regions of superstition. A man, to spare her feelings, conceals and arrests his own progress. And so humanity lingers on its road, as Adam shared the apple, that woman may not be left behind. * *

" It is little wonder that so many of our youth in the passage between the feminine imaginations that have guided their childhood and the actualities of manhood, become hopelessly wrecked and lost for want of sounder knowledge of their own natures and the world's meaning."

—*Edward Maitland.*

Sexual and Health Questions—Light Literature.

"It's Oh! to be a slave
Along with the barbarous Turk,
Where woman has never a soul to save,
If this is Christian work."—Hood.

Heavenly Twins.............................Sarah Grand
Ghosts ....Ibsen
Tess of the D'Urbervilles.....................T. Hardy
Higher Law...................................E. Maitland
By and By...................................   "
Papa's Own Girl........................Marie Howland
Pushed by Unseen Hands..............Helen H. Gardener
Is This Your Son, My Lord?.............   "
Pray You, Sir, Whose Daughter?.........   "
A Thoughtless Yes.....................   "
Anna Karenina.................................Tolstoi
Mother Soul...........................Laura Smith (Greer)
Discords.....................................George Egerton

Heavy Literature.

Prof. Max Muller says: "All truth is safe and nothing else is safe; and he who keeps back the truth or withholds it from men, from motives of expediency, is either a coward or a criminal, or both."

Esoteric Anthropology........................Dr. Nichols
A Vindication of the Rights of Women. Mary Wollstonecraft
Marriage as it was, is, and should be............Mrs. Besant
The Emancipation of Women..................Adele Crepaz
Love's Coming of Age.......................E. Carpenter
The Evolution of Marriage..................Ch. Letourneau
Vindication of Sex.........................Helen Wilmans
British Freewomen..........................Mrs. C. C. Stopes
Education During Sleep..........Sydney H. Flower, LL. D.
Sexual Law and The Philosophy of Perfect Health....Close
Regeneration.................................S. A. Weltmer
Woman......................................August Bebel
Karezza. Ethics of Marriage......Alice B. Stockham, M. D.
Tokology,...........................   "   "   "
Why I Am A Vegetarian................J. Howard Moore
The Nature Cure...............Drs. M. E. and Rosa Conger
American Vegetarian Cookery....................
The True Science of Living....................E. H. Dewey
Perfect Way in Diet.......................Dr. A. B. Kingsford
Physianthropy................Mrs. C. Leigh Hunt Wallace
Physical Culture..........................Carrica LeFavre
The Family Gymnasium.......................T. Trall, M. D.
The Art of Massage........................A. Creighton Hale

THE FAILURE OF THE FINITE TO COM-PREHEND THE INFINITE.

"God called up from dreams a man in the vestibule of Heaven, saying, 'Come thou hither and see the glory of my house.' And to the servants that stood around His throne He said, 'Take him and undress him from his robes of flesh: cleanse his vision, and put a new breath into his nostrils; only touch not with any change his human heart—the heart that weeps and trembles.' It was done: and, with a mighty angel for his guide, the man stood ready for his infinite voyage; and from the terraces of Heaven, without sound or farewell, at once they wheeled away into endless space. Sometimes with the solemn flight of angel wing they fled through Zaarahs of darkness, through wildernesses of death, that divided the worlds of life; sometimes they swept over frontiers, that were quickening under prophetic motions of God. Then, from a distance that is counted only in Heaven, light dawned for a time through a sleepy film; by unutterable pace the light swept to *them:* they, by unutterable pace, to the light. In a moment, the rushing of planets was upon them; in a moment, the blazing of suns was around them.

ꞁ "Then came eternities of twilight, that revealed but were not revealed. On the right hand and on the left, towered mighty constellations, that, by self-repetitions and answers from afar, that by counter-positions, built up triumphal gates, whose architraves, whose archways, horizontal, upright, rested, rose, at altitude by spans that seemed ghostly from infinitude. Without measure were the architraves, past number were the archways, beyond memory the gates. Within were stairs that scaled the eternities below; above was below, below was above, to the man stripped of gravitating body: depth was swallowed up in height insurmountable—height was swallowed up in depth unfathomable. Suddenly, as thus they rode from infinite to infinite, suddenly, as thus they tilted over abysmal worlds, a mighty cry arose, that systems more mysterious,

OCCULT.—Light Literature.

"First slave to words, then vassal to a name,
Then dupe of party; child and man the same:
Bounded by nature, narrowed still by art,
A trifling head and a contracted heart."

Such a condition will prevent the study of these books.

Karma...A. P. Sinnett
The Blossom and the Fruit..................Mabel Collins
The Idyll of the White Lotus................   "
The Coming Race.................................Lytton
A Strange Story...... ....   "
Zanoni..   "
On the Heights of Himalay...............A. Van Der Naillen
The Double Man.................................F. B. Dowd
Nightmare Tales.................................H. P. Blavatsky
The Brother of the Third Degree..............W. L. Garver
Mystery of a Turkish Bath.......................Rita
Mystic Quest......................................Kingland
Magic Skin...Balzac

Heavy Literature.

"Wisdom is the principal thing, therefore get wisdom; and with all
thy getting, get understanding."

Proceedings of the Psychical Research Society..............
Esoteric Buddhism.............................A. P. Sinnett
Occult World...................................   "
The Hasheesh Eater.............................Anonymous
Reincarnation....................................Anderson
The Temple of the Rosy Cross. Part I...........F. B. Dowd
Regeneration. Part II.......   "
Why I Became a Theosophist.......................Besant
In the Outer Court ....   "
Isis Unveiled. 2 vols......................H. P. Blavatsky
Working Glossary for Theosophical Students..............
Psychometry and Thought Transference...................
Ocean of Theosophy..................................Judge
Wilkesbarre Letters on Theosophy.................Fullerton
Rationale of Mesmerism...........................Sinnett
Law of Psychic Phenomena.........................Hudson
Somnambulism.......................Dr. Sydney Flower
How to Hypnotize........................   "
Hypnotism Up To Date.................   "
Moll's Hypnotism......................................
Solar Biology....................................H. E. Butler
Psychometry.........................Joseph R. Buchanan
Automatic or Spirit Writing, Etc........Sara A. Underwood

47

that worlds more billowy, other heights and other depths, were coming, were nearing, were at hand.

"Then the man sighed and stopped, shuddered and wept. His overladen heart uttered itself in tears; and he said, 'Angel, I will go no farther; for the spirit of man acheth with this infinity. Insufferable is the glory of God. Let me lie down in the grave and hide me from the persecution of the infinite; for end I see, there is none.' And from all the listening stars that shone around issued a choral voice, 'The man speaks truly: end there is none, that ever yet we heard of.' 'End is there none?' the angel solemnly demanded: 'Is there indeed no end? and is this the sorrow that kills you?' But no voice answered, that he might answer himself. Then the angel threw up his glorious hands to the Heaven of Heavens, saying, 'End there is none to the universe of God. Lo, also, there is no beginning.'"
—*Jean Paul Richter.*

"The increasing prospect tires the wandering eyes;
  Hill peeps o'er hill and Alps on Alps arise."—*Pope.*

"If ye lay bound upon the wheel of change,
    And no way were of breaking from the chain,
  The Heart of boundless Being is a curse,
    The Soul of Things fell Pain.

"Ye are not bound! the Soul of Things is sweet,
    The Heart of Being is celestial rest;
  Stronger than woe is will: that which was Good
    Doth pass to Better—Best."—*E. Arnold.*

"Yet no man lives, who never, looking backward,
    Sickens at the piteous patchwork all his life will seem,
  When some wind of memory, in his bosom quickens,
    The ashes of ambition, the dust of some dead dream.

"For the Gods gave labor, and failure for its payment;
    The best work in the end seems marred and incomplete,
  Life is a thing of patches, and like to ragged raiment;
    Who will renew the garments, and make the rents to
    meet?"—*Herbert Clarke.*

48

SPIRITUAL AND METAPHYSICAL.

"I form the light, and create darkness: I make peace, and create evil;
I the Lord do all these [things]."—ISAIAH xlv: 7.

Seeking the Kingdom.................................Patterson
Beyond the Clouds................................... "
How We Master Our Fate........................Gestefeld
Breath of Life; Self Treatments................ .... "
The Metaphysics of Balzac.......................... "
The World Beautiful. 3 vols............... ...... Lilian Whiting
The Living Christ......... ....Paul Tyner
The Golden Ladder.......... ....Clarkson
Ideal Suggestion Through Mental Photography......Wood
Studies in the Thought World...................... "
God's Image in Man................................ "
All's Right With the World.............. ....Newcombe
In Tune With the Infinite............ ....Trine
What All the World's A-Seeking................ ...... "
Condensed Thoughts About Christian Science...Holcombe
Power of Thought in Production and Cure Disease "
Influence of Fear in Disease .... "
Power of Silence...............................Dresser
Twelve Lessons in Truth......... ... .Cady
Philosophy of Mental Healing.................. ...... Whipple
Happiness as Found in Forethought Minus Fearthought.
....Fletcher
Menticulture; the A B C of True Living........... "
Dr. Geo. Foote on Mental Healing........................
Old and New Psychology.......................Colville
Healing Thoughts....................................Barton
The Mastery of Fate. 2 vols.......................Braun
Power Through Repose.................Annie Payson Call
Don't Worry; The Scientific Law of Happiness.....Seward
Big Truths for Little People.......................Cramer
The Law of Vibrations..............................Shelton
Vibrations; The Law of Life......................Williams
Science and Healing.........................M. E. Cramer
In Search of a Soul..............................Dresser
Perfect Whole..................................... "
Spiritual Consciousness.................Frank H. Sprague
Suggestive Therapeutics.................... .....Bernheim
Psycho Therapeutics.......................Lloyd Tuckey
Science and Health.......................Mary B. G. Eddy
Mental Medicine.............................W. F. Evans
Primitive Mind Cure................................ "
Esoteric Christianity and Mental Therapeutics "
Divine Law of Cure............................... "

"Men of large mind are very rarely happy men. It is your little animal-minded individual who can be happy. *Thus women, who reflect less,* are as a class happier and more contented than men. But the large-minded man sees too far, and guesses too much of what he cannot see. He looks forward, and notes the dusty end of his laborious days; he looks around and shudders at the unceasing misery of a coarse struggling world; the sight of the pitiful beggar babe craving bread on tottering feet pierces his heart. He cannot console himself with the reflection that the child had no business to be born, or that if he denuded himself of his last dollar he would not materially help the class which bred it. * * * For such a man, in such a mood, even religion has terrors as well as hopes, and while the gloom gathers about his mind these are with him more and more. What lies beyond that arching mystery to whose horizon he draws daily more close—whose doors may even now be opening for him? A hundred voices answer, but no two agree. A hundred hands point out a hundred roads to knowledge—they are lost half way."—*H. Rider Haggard.*

"Remember:—It is not the act, but the will, which marks the soul of the man. He who has crushed a nation sins no more than he who rejoices in the death throe of the meanest creature. The stagnant pool is not less poisonous drop for drop than the mighty swamp, though its reach is smaller. He who has desired to be and accomplish what this man has been and accomplished, is as this man; though he have lacked the power to perform."—*Olive Schreiner.*

"On the other hand we must not forget that we are in action individually controlled by the laws we make collectively. If the laws made collectively are evil, the individual no matter how well disposed will have to express himself in an evil manner, until the laws are changed."
—*Walter L. Sinton.*

"Circumstances govern all without, character all within."
—*E. Maitland.*

HELEN WILMAN'S PUBLICATIONS.

The Blossom of the Century. This is a mental science book; it is all about the possibilities of human power; the power vested in human development. It is at once a mighty revelation and a mightier prophecy. Such a book is inestimable in iis capacity to unfold native mental ability in the person who studies it and to establish him in unfaltering self trust; the absence of self trust is self defeat every time; its absence is the curse of the race; it is neither poverty nor disease nor oppression that curses us; it is the want of self confidence that does it. The man who has self trust goes up head; those who lack it take their places below him and stand, usually, where the self trustful man places him.

Wilman's Express Condensed. Consists of two volumes of Essays by Helen Wilmans and Ada Wilmans Powers. They have had a large sale and have been extravagantly praised.

Poverty and Its Cure. It will prove a sure way out of the thralls to those who will study it thoroughly.

Vindication of Sex. This is a powerfully written treatise upon a subject now occuqying the world's thought to a greater extedt than any other. Sex is the basis of all life; and yet nothing is so abused, maligned and misunderstood.

Home Course in Mental Science. Twenty lessons in twenty pamphlets: 1, Omnipresent Life. 2, Thought, the Body-Builder. 3, Our Beliefs. 4, Denials. 5, Affirmations. 6, The Soul of Things. 7, Faith, Our Guide Through the Dark. 8, Spirit and Body are One. 9, Prayer and Self Culture. 10, The Power Behind the Throne. 11, The Power Above the Throne. 12, The Ling on His Throne. 13, Mental Science a Race Movement. 14, Mental Science Incarnate in Flesh and Blood. 15, Personality and Individuality. 16, "The Stone that the Builders Rejected." 17, A Noble Egoism the Foundation of Just Action. 18, Recognitien of the Will the Cure of Disease. 19, Practical Healing. 20, Posture of the Will Man.

A Search for Freedom.

A Healing Formula.

"Freedom." A twelve page weekly paper, edited by Helen Wilmans.

51

" When the bread is bitter, it is easy not to linger at the meal. When the oil is low, it is easy to rise with the dawn. When the body is without surfeit or temptation, it is easy to rise above flesh on the wings of the spirit. You say poverty is very terrible to you and kills the soul in you, but is it not like the northern blast, which lashes men into vikings? is it not the luscious south wind, which lulls them into lotus eaters?"—*Ouida.*

" If thy success had been greater, thou hadst been less."

> " By thine own soul's law, learn to live,
> And if men thwart thee take no heed,
> And if men hate thee have no care;
> Live thou thy life and do thy deed,
> Hope thou thy hope and pray thy prayer,
> And ask no meed they will not give."

" This above all:—to thine own self be true,
And it must follow, as the night the day,
Thou canst not then be false to any man."

> " And for success I ask no more than this—
> To bear unflinching witness to the Truth."
> " No!
> True freedom is to share
> All the chains our brothers wear,
> And with hand and heart to be
> Earnest to make others free!"—*Lowell.*

" The problem which every honest man has to face, is not one of more or less bread and butter, but of THE RIGHT TO DO RIGHT. As to any individual being honest in practice under the present commercial system, it is utterly impossible. There is no position in which we could be placed, in which we should be independent of our fellows, and if such a position were possible, it would not be right for us to occupy it, as we owe a debt to our forefathers, which we must liquidate by carrying on the work that they commenced to its final completion, viz.:—the ultimate freedom of all mankind *to do right.*"—*W. L. Sinton.*

WHITE CROSS LIBRARY.

By PRENTICE MULFORD.

Is a system of publication, showing how results may be obtained in all business and art, through the force of thought and silent power of mind.

VOLUME I.

You Travel When You Sleep.
Where You Travel When You Sleep.
The Process of Re-embodiment.
Re-embodiment Universal in Nature.
The Art of Forgetting.
How Thoughts Are Born.
The Law of Success.
How to Keep Your Strength.
Consider the Lilies.
Art of Study.
Profit and Loss in Associates.
The Slavery of Fear.
What are Spiritual Gifts.

VOLUME II.

Some Laws of Health and Beauty,
Mental Intemperance.
Law of Marriage.
The God in Yourself.
Force, and How to Get It.
The Doctor Within.
Co-operation of Thought.
The Religion of Dress.
The Necessity of Riches.
Use Your Riches.
The Healing and Renewing Force of Spring.
Positive and Negative Thought.

VOLUME III.

The Practical use of Reverie.
Your two Memories.
Self Teaching; or the art of Learning how to
    Learn.
How to Push Your Business.
The Religion of the Drama.
The Uses of Sickness.
Who are our Relations?
The Use of a Room.
Man and Wife.
Cure for Alcoholic Intemperance.
The Church of Silent Demand.
The Mystery of Sleep, or our Double Existence.

" Thou great eternal Infinite; the great unbounded whole.
Thy body is the universe, Thy spirit is the soul.
If thou dost fill immensity, if thou art all in all,
If thou wert here before I was, I am not here at all.
How could I live outside of thee? Dost thou fill earth and air?
There surely is no place for me outside of everywhere.
If thou art God and thou dost fill immensity of space,
Then I am God, think as you will, or else I have no place.
And if I have no place at all, or if I am not here,
' Banished' I surely cannot be, for then I'd be somewhere.
Then I must be a part of God, no matter if I'm small,
And if I'm not a part of Him, there's no such God at all."
                                                —*Anon.*

" Love, hope, aud joy, fair pleasure's smiling train,
    Hate, fear, and grief, the family of pain;
    These mixed with art, and to due bounds confined,
    Make and maintain the balance of the mind;
    The lights and shades, whose well accorded strife
    Gives all the strength and color of our life."—*Pope.*

    " Ever at toil, it brings to loveliness
        All ancient wrath and wreck."—*E. Arnold.*

FOUR CLASSES OF MEN.

" He that knows not and knows not that he knows
not, he is a fool; shun him.
" He that knows not, and knows that he knows not,
he is simple; teach him.
" He that knows and knows not that he knows, he is
asleep; wake him.
" He that knows and knows that he knows, he is wise;
follow him."   —*Author Unknown.*

    " To will what God doth will,
        That is the only Science
        Doth give us any rest."—*Longfellow.*

54

VOLUME IV.

The Use of Sunday.
The Drawing Power of Mind.
Grace Before Meat; or Science of Eating.
The Source of Your Strength.
What We Need Strength For.
One Way to Cultivate Courage.
The Material Mind vs. The Spiritual Mind.
Marriage and Resurrection.
Immortality in the Flesh.
Faith; or, Being Led of the Spirit.
Some Practical Mental Recipes.
The Use and Necessity of Recreation.

VOLUME V.

Mental Tyranny.
Spells; or, The Law of Change.
Look Forward.
Thought Currents.
Healthy and Unhealthy Spirit Communion.
Uses of Diversion.
Regeneration; or, Being Born Again.
Lies Breed Disease; Truths Bring Health.
God's Commands are Man's Demands.
About Economizing our Forces.
God in the Trees, or the Infinite Mind in Nature.
What is Justice?

VOLUME VI.

Woman's Real Power.
Love Thyself.
About Prentice Mulford.
Mental Medicine.
Prayer in all Ages.
The Attraction of Aspiration.
Cultivate Repose.
Good and Ill Effects of Thought.
Buried Talents.
The Power of Honesty.
Confession.
The Accession of New Thought.

These six volumes embrace and conclude the entire series.

The Swamp Angel.

Prentice Mulford's Story. (36 chapters—300 pa

"Duty rises at first, a gloomy tyranny, out of man's helplessness, his self mistrust, in a word, his abstract fear. He personifies all that he abstractly fears as God, and straightway becomes the slave of his duty to God. He imposes that slavery fiercely on his children, threatening them with hell, and punishing them for their attempts to be happy. When, becoming bolder, he ceases to fear everything, and dares to love something, this duty of his to what he fears evolves into a sense of duty to what he loves. Sometimes he again personifies what he loves as God; and the God of Wrath becomes the God of Love: sometimes he at once becomes a humanitarian, an altruist, acknowledging only his duty to his neighbor. This stage is correlative to the rationalist stage in the evolution of philosophy and the capitalist*phase in the evolution of industry. But in it the emancipated slave of God falls under the dominion of society, which, having just reached a phase in which all the love is ground out of it by the competitive struggle for money, remorselessly crushes him, until in due course of the further growth of his spirit or will, a sense at last arises in him of his duty to himself. And when this sense is fully grown, which it hardly is yet, the tyranny of duty is broken; for now the man's God is himself; and he, self satisfied at last, ceases to be selfish. The evangelist of this last step must therefore preach the repudiation of duty. This, to the unprepared of his generation, is indeed the wanton masterpiece of paradox. What! after all that has been said by men of noble life as to the secret of all right conduct being only ' Duty, duty, duty,' is he to be told now that duty is the primal curse from which we must redeem ourselves before we can advance another step along which, as we imagine—having forgotten the repudiations made by our fathers—duty and duty alone has brought us thus far? But why not?

"The idealist higher in the ascent of evolution than the Philistine, yet hates the highest and strikes at him with a dread and rancor of which the easy going Philistine is guiltless. The man who has risen above the danger and

*More scientifically speaking, monopolist.

56

SPIRITUAL—Light Literature.

"He who knows only one Religion, knows none."—PROF. MAX MULLER.

"From Nature up to Law, from Law to Love,
This, the ascendent path in which we move,
Impelled by God in ways that lighten still,
Till all things meet in one eternal thrill."
—BISHOP OF PEORIA, in "Means and Ends of Education."

David Elginbrod...... ....George MacDonald
The Elect Lady........................... "
What's Mine's Mine.................... "
Ardath....................................... Marie Corelli
The Sorrows of Satan........................ "
Les Miserables................................ Victor Hugo
Dreams and Dream Stories.............. Anna B. Kingsford
The Christian.................................. Hall Caine

Heavy Literature.

"To love is to live;
To love one's self is to live in Hell;
To love another is to live on Earth;
To love others is to live in Heaven;
To silently adore the self in all creatures is to live in that self which is
eternal peace."—BISHOP OF PEORIA, in "Means and Ends of Education."

"No man can be brave who thinks pain the greatest evil; nor temper-
ate who considers pleasure the highest good."—CICERO.

The Life of the Harp in the Hands of the Harper..Schlatter
The Spirit Wrestlers or Doukhoborki...Vladimir Tchertkoff
John Woodman's Journal.......................... Whittier
History of the Quakers.............................. ....
The Light of Asia .... E. Arnold
Life and Love and Death........................... B. Hall
Things as They Are.................................. "
The Story of the New Gospel of Interpretation..E. Maitland
The New Gospel of Interpretation.............. "
Civilization; Its Cause and Cure.............. E. Carpenter
Towards Democracy........................... "
Emerson's Essays.................................... ......
Sartor Resartus.................................... Carlyle
The Way, the Truth and the Life........... ....J. H. Dewey
The Pathway of the Spirit..................... "
Bhagavad Gita.................................... ....
ThePerfect Way, or the Finding of Christ....A. B. Kingsford
Clothed With the Sun........................ "
Raga Yoga Lectures.................. Swami Vivekananda
Magic White and Black............ Franz Hartmann, M. D.
Life of Jehoshua...................... " "
Light on the Path.......................... Mabel Collins

the fear that his acquisitiveness will lead him to theft, his temper to murder, and his affections to debauchery: this is he who is denounced as an arch scoundrel and libertine, and thus confounded with the lowest because he is the highest. And it is not the ignorant and stupid who maintain this error, but the literate and the cultured. When the true prophet speaks, he is proved to be both rascal and idiot, not by those who have never read how foolishly such learned demonstrations have come off in the past, but by those who have themselves written volumes on the crucifixions, the burnings, the stonings, the headings and the hangings, the Siberian transportations, the calumny and ostracism, which have been the lot of the pioneer as well as of the camp follower." —*Bernard Shaw.*

ABOU BEN ADHEM AND THE ANGEL.

"Abou Ben Adhem (may his tribe increase)
Awoke one night from a deep dream of peace,
And saw within the moonlight in his room,
Making it rich, and like a lily in bloom,
An angel, writing in a book of gold:—
Exceeding peace had made Ben Adhem bold,
And to the presence in the room he said,
'What writest thou?' The vision raised its head,
And, with a look made of all sweet accord,
Answered, 'The names of those who love the Lord.'
'And is mine one?' said Abou: 'Nay, not so,'
Replied the angel. Abou spoke more low,
But cheerily still; and said, 'I pray thee then,
Write me as one that loves his fellow men.'
The angel wrote, and vanished. The next night
It came again with a great wakening light,
And showed the names whom love of God had blest,
And lo! Ben Adhem's name led all the rest."
—*Leigh Hunt.*

"We are born into conditions escape from which is hopeless and continuance in which is intolerable."

58

MISCELLANEOUS.

"May liberty meet wi' success,
May prudence protect her fra evil;
May tyrants and tyranny tire in the mist,
And wander their way to the de'vil.
Here's freedom to him that would read.
Here's freedom to him that would write;
There's none are afeard
That the truth should be heerd,
But they whom the truth would indict."—BURNS.

"All nature is but Art, unknown to thee;
All chance, direction which thou canst not see;
All discord, harmony not understood;
All partial evil, universal good;
And, spite of Pride, in erring Reason's spite,
One truth is clear, Whatever is is right."—POPE,

The Labor Annual ....
Finance and Transportation.....................J. D. Miller
Hell To Pay.......................................Mayor Jones
President John Smith...
Argument of Clarence S. Darrow in the Wood-Workers Con-
　spiracy Case..
Live Questions.....................Ex-Gov. John P. Altgeld
The State Carriage, with Chart ....Timewell
How to Get Rich Without Working........E. Homer Bailey
The Rights of Woman and the Sexual Relation...K. Heinzen
My Confession, My Religion. Life....................Tolstoi
A Persian Pearl and Other Essays......Clarence S. Darrow
My Soul and Winter's...............Laura Smith (Greer)
The Keys of the Creeds.........................E. Maitland
Tales of Two Countries................Alexander Kielland
Ten Tales.............................Francois Coppee
The Day's Work.....................................Kipling
Harmonics of Evolution..................Florence Huntley
Dream Child.."
A Traveler from Altruria............William Dean Howells
The Mystery of the Ages.............Countess of Caithness
The Soul of a People.....................H. Fielding
Selections from Geo. MacDonald, or Helps for Weary Souls
Hours With the Mystics. 2 vols. in 1..........R. A. Vaughn
Dreams..Schreiner
Adam's Peak to Elephanta.....................E. Carpenter
Treasury of the Humble...............Maurice Maeterlinck
Wisdom and Destiny Essays,.......... "
The World's Congress of Religions.......................
Seven Creative Principles......................H. E. Butler
Message of the Mystics.......................Mary H. Ford
The Spirit of the New Testament.............By a Woman

A CURE FOR A CONSCIENCE.

There was a Man who was troubled with a conscience. He felt that his life was not what it ought to be. Therefore he resorted to the physicians He asked a statesman if politics would agree with his conscience. The statesman replied that conscience had a place in politics, but that, if we followed conscience, we could accomplish nothing; for in politics, obedience to the moral law is an iridescent dream.

"We must," he explained, "discover the best issue presented, and vote for that, though it be not abstractly right, else we shall throw away our votes. If we act thus, we may not only serve the state, but attain to office." The Man said, "I like not the morality of the politician." (This Man was a dangerous man.) The Man then asked a high priest if his conscience could be made useful, and the priest answered: "Yes, man is nothing without a conscience—on Sunday; on week days it were well for him to leave it in church." The priest added, "The teachings of Christ are counsels of perfection. If everyone would obey them you also might do so, but here you must act as best you can, and if you do your best it will be all right with you in the next world." "But," said the Man, "I live in this world."

The Man asked a man of this world what he should do with his unsatisfied conscience. The captain of industry answered: "You would better put your conscience in cold storage. The laws of business and the penal code embody the moral law; you have only to follow them. If your conscience is uneasy, smash it with the ledger and heap upon it the revised statutes. So may you get rich." And the Man with a conscience went away sorrowful, for he had much conviction. Yet was the Man not discouraged. He asked the theologians, and they answered variously: "If you would have peace—believe," "sacrifice," "work," "fast." And nearly all said "give," but not even one said "love."

Then the Man went to a prophet of God, and the prophet said: "Seek first the Kingdom." The Man asked, "Shall I get high office thereby?" "You will be a servant

POETRY.

"Poets are all who love who feel great truths,
And tell them; for the truth of truths is love."
—PHILIP JAMES BAILEY.

"Love is the highest attribute of Deity;
And he who loves divinely is most blest.
It purgeth passion from the soul and sense,
And makes the man a unit in himself;
Head, eyes, hands, heart, all work in unison,
And beasts and savages, and rudest hinds,
All feel alike its exercise of power.

Ambition cannot walk with it; for he
Who learns to live and love aright, loves all,
And finds preferment in the general weal.
Though, Proteus like, it takes a thousand forms,
It doth o'ercome all evil with its good.
Casteth out devils,—sensuality, and sin,
And green-eyed jealousy, and hate; and like
Chrysostom, golden-mouthed, it doth attune
The words of common speech to sweet accord,
And give significance to simplest things."
—LIZZIE DOTEN.

"O, my mortal friends and brothers!
We are each and all another's,
And the soul that gives most freely from its treasure hath the more;
Would you lose your life, you find it,
And in giving love you bind it
Like an amulet of safety to your heart forevermore."
—LIZZIE DOTEN.

Charles Mackie's Poems   Lowell's Poetical Works
  Burns' Poetical Works   Rudyard Kipling's Poems
Lizzie Doten's Poems from the Inner Life
  Walt Whitman's Poems   Whittier's Poetical Works
Lewis Morris' Poems   William Morris' Poems
  Gerald Massey's Poems   Sam Walter Foss' Poems
New Ballads, Ballads and Songs, by John Davidson
  Fleet Eclogues, by Davidson   Helen Jackson's Poems
In This Our World, by Charlotte Perkins Stetson
                    Young Ofeg's Ditties, by Ola Hansen
          Ella Wheeler Wilcox's Poems

"The virtues of society are the vices of the saint."—EMERSON.

of servants." "Shall I get riches?" "You must leave all to follow the light." "Shall I have quiet of mind?" "It is written, 'I come not to bring peace, but a sword.'" "What then do you offer me if I seek the kingdom?" "I offer you only love for men and the joy of the spiritual life." The Man said: "The road to the Kingdom is dark." And the prophet answered, "But the light is within you, for it is written, 'The path of the just is as a shining light, that shineth more and more unto the perfect day.'"

—*Bolton Hall.*

BEWARE.

Have you always been respected by your neighbors?

Do they ask your advice on all important matters?

Do they all speak well of you and point you out as a leading citizen and a pillar of society?

Has no one ever said that you were beside yourself,

Or called you crazy, or a crank, or a pestilent fellow?

Have you never been accused of associating with publicans and sinners, or of stirring up the people, or of turning the world upside down?

In short, are you thoroughly respectable?

Then beware; you are on the downward road; you are in bad company.

Mend your ways or you can claim no kinship with the saints and heroes which were before you.

—*Ernest H. Crosby.*